Aircraft Expen$e Tracking

Aircraft Owner's Expense and
Maintenance Tracking System
Single Engine (SE) or
Multi Engine (ME)
Sole Ownership or Club

For the year 20___

James D. Price
ATP, CFII / MEI
Retired Airline Captain
Colonel, USAFR (Retired)

http://www.JDPriceCFI.com

This publication is printed for informational purposes only and is not intended to substitute for any aircraft or personal logbook. Consult the IRS or your accountant for more information. The experts are better qualified to answer questions based on your individual circumstances.

Limitation of Liability

This information is provided solely for your individual, non-commercial use. There are no representations or warranties of any kind made pertaining to this service or information. Under no circumstances or theories of liability, including without limitation the negligence of any party, contract, warranty or strict liability in tort, shall the author or any of its affiliated or related organizations be liable for any direct, indirect, incidental, special, consequential or punitive damages as a result of the use of, or the inability to use, any information provided through this book.

ISBN 978-1-938586-80-4

Printed in the United States of America
Writers Cramp Publishing
http://www.writerscramp.us

Other books by James D. Price

Flight Review Study Guide will be the first thing you open when getting ready for any pilot proficiency training. Wings flights, or BFR. – everything is covered. **Flight Review Study Guide** is also an indispensable cross county flight-planning handbook. You'll fly with confidence and you'll be a better pilot.

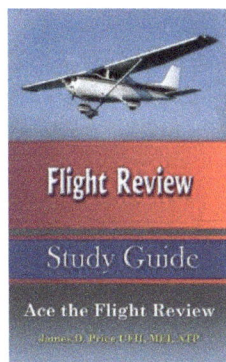

ISBN 978-1-938586-81-1

Instrument Proficiency Check Study Guide contains the insight of a professional pilot. Let Jim's training and teaching experiences help you prepare for the IPC. Crack this open any time you need to brush up on your instrument skills and knowledge. It will instill a sense of confidence that only in-depth knowledge can bring. It's a quick and easy way to ACE the IPC.

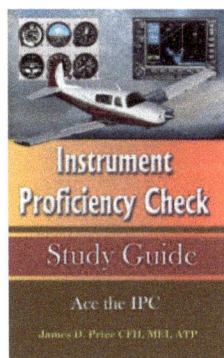

ISBN 978-1-938586-82-8

For more information or to chat with Jim, visit his website at:
http://www.JDPriceCFI.com

Printed in the U.S.A.
http://www.WritersCramp.us

Whether the aircraft is all yours, or it's part of a partnership, or club; SEL or MEL, reciprocating or turbine – this tool is for you. When is that engine due for an oil change? You'll quickly see it in *"Aircraft Expen$e Tracking"*.

I don't make jokes. I just watch the government and report the facts.
-Will Rogers

Designed to help aircraft owners keep an accurate record of expenses, *"Tracking"* simplifies efforts and minimizes tax time pain. In addition, aircraft owners can easily keep a running total of maintenance and navigation costs, breaking down business and charity flight hours and their operating costs.

"Aircraft Expen$e Tracking" does not replace FAA required logbooks, but it sure makes your life easier. It's a cost based accounting system with reminders for Instrument, Avionics, Engine and Airframe repairs, AD's and SB's.

Using This Book

Use it for SEL/MEL aircraft with reciprocating or turbine engines; sole ownership, partnership, or a club aircraft. *It's designed to:*

- o Help aircraft owners keep an accurate record of expenses; simplifying efforts at tax time.
- o Help aircraft owners keep a running total of maintenance and navigation costs, breaking down business flight and charity flight hours and operating costs.

When you fly for business, in addition to the date, time and destination, you should note the PURPOSE of the trip, the NAME OF THE PERSON MET, and a DESCRIPTION OF THE WORK PERFORMED. Don't be brief when it comes to tax records. Record each leg of a business or a charity flight in detail.

Date:	*8*	End Time:	*2440.0*	Bus Hours	Charity Hours
From:	*VNY*	Start Time:	*2437.0*		
To:	*PHX*	*Met w/ A. Lincoln* Tot: *3.0*		*3.0*	
Date:	*8*	End Time:	*2443.5*	Bus Hours	Charity Hours
From:	*PHX*	Start Time:	*2440.0*		
To:	*VNY*	*Job Proposal* Tot: *3.5*		*3.5*	

This book will help you keep track of:

- o Oil usage (helps alert you of impending engine problems).
- o VOR checks
- o GPS database updates

CAUTION, this book is not a substitute for an engine or aircraft logbook. *It will, however, help you track:*

- o Aircraft squawks
- o Impending maintenance and oil changes
- o Parts replacements
- o Overhauls
- o ADs

Keep this book in the aircraft where you can access it easily. Enter the flight time, tie-down fees, fuel and oil purchases/usage, maintenance costs, wash jobs, etc. If a particular trip has eight legs, the entire non-business or charity flight can be summarized on one or two lines. This helps conserve space for other trips in the month.

If you keep it up to date and complete a Year-to-Date Summary each month, you'll find that the year-end summary, (located on the last page), will be extremely easy.

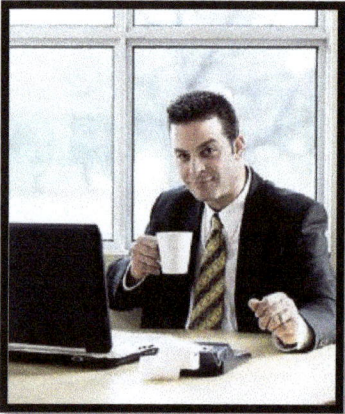

The Year-End Summary is designed to be tax season and accountant ready. If you have questions about tax laws, check with your accountant or the IRS.

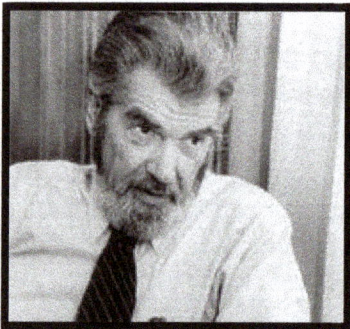

"Few of us ever test our powers of deduction, except when filling out an income tax form."

Laurence J. Peter, author of *"The Peter Principle"*

Aircraft & Owner Data

Owner Data
Name:
Address:
City and State:
Phone:
e-mail:

Aircraft Data for:	
Make	**Model**
Year	**Serial Number**
TTSN (Total time Since New):	

L - Engine	**L - Serial Number**
L – SMOH (Since Major Overhaul)	**L – STOH** (Since Top Overhaul)
Overhaul due:	
R - Engine	**R - Serial Number**
R – SMOH	**R - STOH**
Overhaul due:	
L - Prop	**Serial Number**
Overhauled at (time):	
R - Prop	**Serial Number**
Overhauled at (time):	

Gross Wt	Empty Wt	Useful Load

Fuel gal.	Fuel lb.	

OIL Brand & Weight	
Winter Oil	
Summer Oil	

	Tires			Installation	
	Make	Size	Inflation	Date	Hours
L Main					
R Main					
Nose/Tail					

Inspections	Date of Inspection	Due Date
Annual		(+12 Mo.)
ELT		(+24 Mo.)
Static		(+24 Mo.)
Transponder		(+24 Mo.)

Professionals	Name	Phone
Mechanic		
Avionics		

Personal		
Medical Date	BFR Date	IPC Date
Expires	Expires	Expires

Part Replacement Schedule

Parts Requiring Replacement			
Part	Hours or months before replacement:	Last installed, date & TT:	Due for replacement @:

Insurance Agency		
Policy No.	Agent	Phone #
Coverage:		

Squawk Sheet

Discrepancy	DATE ENTERED	DATE RESOLVED

Squawk Sheet

Discrepancy	DATE ENTERED	DATE RESOLVED

ADs			
#	Subject	Date Complied	Due next at:

Service Bulletins

#	Date Complied	Subject

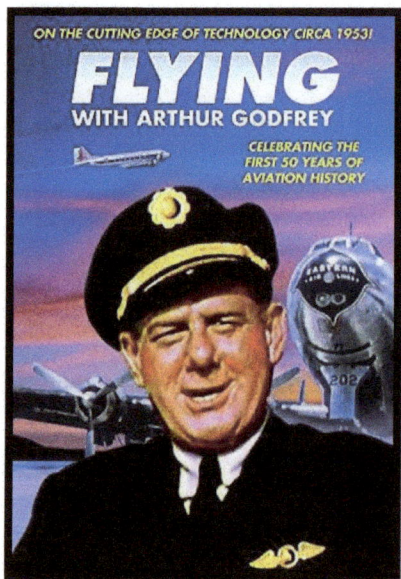

"I'm proud to be paying taxes in the United States. The only thing is – I could be just a proud for half of the money."

Arthur Godfrey, American radio and television broadcaster, entertainer, and pilot

Maintenance & Navigation Costs

- Inspecting and repairing the aircraft, including ADs and Service Bulletins
- Inspecting and repairing avionics
- Maintaining the GPS database for IFR currency
- Maintaining a VFR and IFR library of charts
- Subscriptions to Jeppesen, AOPA, etc.
- Purchasing flight planning software or subscriptions to flight planning web sites, etc.

Accept that some days you're the pigeon and some days you're the statue. Anon

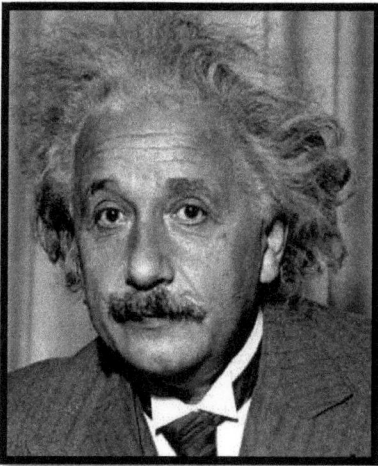

Albert Einstein
On taxes: *"The hardest thing in the world to understand is the income tax."*

On filing a tax return: *"This is too difficult for a mathematician. It takes a philosopher."*

Instrument Repairs/Replacements & Static 24 month inspections

Date	Hours	Item	$
		Total Cost	

Avionics Repairs/Replacements & Transponder 24 month inspections			
Date	Hours	Item	$
		Total Cost	

Engine and Prop ADs, Repairs & Replacement Costs			
Date	Hours	Item & which engine?	$
		Total Cost	

Airframe ADs, Repairs/Replacements, Service Bulletins, 100 Hr and Annual Inspection Costs			
Date	Hours	Item	$
		Total Cost	

GPS Internal Software Updates		
Date	Revision / Version No.	$
	Total Cost	

GPS 28 Day Jeppesen Database Updates		
Individual or Yearly Subscriptions		
Date	Revision / Version No.	$
	Total Cost	

Navigation: VFR/IFR Charts and Approach Plates

Date	Revision / Version No.	$
	Total Cost	

Subscriptions - Jeppesen, AOPA, Flight Planning Software, Web Sites, etc.

Date	Revision / Version No.	$
	Total Cost	

Q 1 Monthly Flight Hours, Fuel and Oil Expenses, Oil Use Log, VOR Checks and GPS Database Updates

Q 1 *Oil Record*

Left Engine (or only engine) Oil Record			
Oil Changed @ Hrs:			
Oil Brand and Weight			
Next Oil Change Due:			
Qt(s) added	Brand & Weight added	@ Tach / Hobbs	Engine Hrs per Qt

Right Engine Oil Record			
Oil Changed @ Hrs:			
Oil Brand and Weight			
Next Oil Change Due:			
Qt(s) added	Brand & Weight added	@ Tach / Hobbs	Engine Hrs per Qt

January

Date:		End Time:		Bus Hours	Charity Hours
From:		Start Time:			
To:			Tot:		
Date:		End Time:		Bus Hours	Charity Hours
From:		Start Time:			
To:			Tot:		
Date:		End Time:		Bus Hours	Charity Hours
From:		Start Time:			
To:			Tot:		
Date:		End Time:		Bus Hours	Charity Hours
From:		Start Time:			
To:			Tot:		
Date:		End Time:		Bus Hours	Charity Hours
From:		Start Time:			
To:			Tot:		
Date:		End Time:		Bus Hours	Charity Hours
From:		Start Time:			
To:			Tot:		
Date:		End Time:		Bus Hours	Charity Hours
From:		Start Time:			
To:			Tot:		
Date:		End Time:		Bus Hours	Charity Hours
From:		Start Time:			
To:			Tot:		
Date:		End Time:		Bus Hours	Charity Hours
From:		Start Time:			
To:			Tot:		
Date:		End Time:		Bus Hours	Charity Hours
From:		Start Time:			
To:			Tot:		

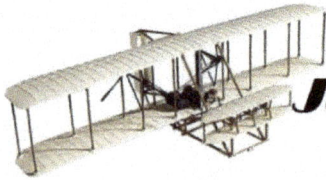

January

Date:		End Time:		Bus Hours	Charity Hours
From:		Start Time:			
To:			Tot:		
Date:		End Time:		Bus Hours	Charity Hours
From:		Start Time:			
To:			Tot:		
Date:		End Time:		Bus Hours	Charity Hours
From:		Start Time:			
To:			Tot:		
Date:		End Time:		Bus Hours	Charity Hours
From:		Start Time:			
To:			Tot:		
Date:		End Time:		Bus Hours	Charity Hours
From:		Start Time:			
To:			Tot:		
Date:		End Time:		Bus Hours	Charity Hours
From:		Start Time:			
To:			Tot:		
Date:		End Time:		Bus Hours	Charity Hours
From:		Start Time:			
To:			Tot:		
Date:		End Time:		Bus Hours	Charity Hours
From:		Start Time:			
To:			Tot:		
Date:		End Time:		Bus Hours	Charity Hours
From:		Start Time:			
To:			Tot:		

January & Year to Date Summary of Hours

	Business	Charity	Total
January:			

DATE			TOTAL GALS	FUEL COST	QTS OIL		OIL COST
	Airfield	$/Gal			L	R	

JANUARY EXPENSES

January Fuel & Oil TOTALS:						

January Charity - Fuel & Oil Costs:

DATE	OTHER EXPENSES (Ramp, O$_2$, Oil change, etc.)	COST

FIXED EXPENSES	
Hangar	
Insurance	
Loan	

GRAND TOTAL COST FOR January

FLIGHT HOURS / FUEL COST SUMMARY TO DATE				
	HOURS	GALS FUEL	FUEL COST	FUEL COST PER HR
Jan YTD:				

VOR Check (every 30 days, FAR 91.171)		
Date & signature	Location & Method	Error or Bearing

GPS Database Updates (AIM 1-1-19)			
REV #	EFFECTIVE	EXPIRES	INSTALL DATE

February

Date:		End Time:		Bus Hours	Charity Hours
From:		Start Time:			
To:			Tot:		
Date:		End Time:		Bus Hours	Charity Hours
From:		Start Time:			
To:			Tot:		
Date:		End Time:		Bus Hours	Charity Hours
From:		Start Time:			
To:			Tot:		
Date:		End Time:		Bus Hours	Charity Hours
From:		Start Time:			
To:			Tot:		
Date:		End Time:		Bus Hours	Charity Hours
From:		Start Time:			
To:			Tot:		
Date:		End Time:		Bus Hours	Charity Hours
From:		Start Time:			
To:			Tot:		
Date:		End Time:		Bus Hours	Charity Hours
From:		Start Time:			
To:			Tot:		
Date:		End Time:		Bus Hours	Charity Hours
From:		Start Time:			
To:			Tot:		
Date:		End Time:		Bus Hours	Charity Hours
From:		Start Time:			
To:			Tot:		
Date:		End Time:		Bus Hours	Charity Hours
From:		Start Time:			
To:			Tot:		

February

Date:		End Time:		Bus Hours	Charity Hours
From:		Start Time:			
To:			Tot:		
Date:		End Time:		Bus Hours	Charity Hours
From:		Start Time:			
To:			Tot:		
Date:		End Time:		Bus Hours	Charity Hours
From:		Start Time:			
To:			Tot:		
Date:		End Time:		Bus Hours	Charity Hours
From:		Start Time:			
To:			Tot:		
Date:		End Time:		Bus Hours	Charity Hours
From:		Start Time:			
To:			Tot:		
Date:		End Time:		Bus Hours	Charity Hours
From:		Start Time:			
To:			Tot:		
Date:		End Time:		Bus Hours	Charity Hours
From:		Start Time:			
To:			Tot:		
Date:		End Time:		Bus Hours	Charity Hours
From:		Start Time:			
To:			Tot:		
Date:		End Time:		Bus Hours	Charity Hours
From:		Start Time:			
To:			Tot:		

February & Year to Date Summary of Hours			
	Business	Charity	Total
February:			
Jan:			
YTD:			

| DATE | | | TOTAL GALS | FUEL COST | QTS OIL | | OIL COST |
	Airfield	$/Gal			L	R	

FEBRUARY EXPENSES

February Fuel & Oil TOTALS:				
February Charity - Fuel & Oil Costs:				

DATE	OTHER EXPENSES (Ramp, O_2, Oil change, etc.)	COST
	FIXED EXPENSES	
	Hangar	
	Insurance	
	Loan	
	GRAND TOTAL COST FOR February	

FLIGHT HOURS / FUEL COST SUMMARY TO DATE				
	HOURS	GALS FUEL	FUEL COST	FUEL COST PER HR
February:				
+Jan:				
YTD:				

VOR Check (every 30 days, FAR 91.171)		
Date & signature	Location & Method	Error or Bearing

GPS Database Updates (AIM 1-1-19)			
REV #	EFFECTIVE	EXPIRES	INSTALL DATE

March

Date:		End Time:		Bus Hours	Charity Hours
From:		Start Time:			
To:			Tot:		
Date:		End Time:		Bus Hours	Charity Hours
From:		Start Time:			
To:			Tot:		
Date:		End Time:		Bus Hours	Charity Hours
From:		Start Time:			
To:			Tot:		
Date:		End Time:		Bus Hours	Charity Hours
From:		Start Time:			
To:			Tot:		
Date:		End Time:		Bus Hours	Charity Hours
From:		Start Time:			
To:			Tot:		
Date:		End Time:		Bus Hours	Charity Hours
From:		Start Time:			
To:			Tot:		
Date:		End Time:		Bus Hours	Charity Hours
From:		Start Time:			
To:			Tot:		
Date:		End Time:		Bus Hours	Charity Hours
From:		Start Time:			
To:			Tot:		
Date:		End Time:		Bus Hours	Charity Hours
From:		Start Time:			
To:			Tot:		
Date:		End Time:		Bus Hours	Charity Hours
From:		Start Time:			
To:			Tot:		

March

Date:		End Time:		Bus	Charity
From:		Start Time:		Hours	Hours
To:			Tot:		
Date:		End Time:		Bus	Charity
From:		Start Time:		Hours	Hours
To:			Tot:		
Date:		End Time:		Bus	Charity
From:		Start Time:		Hours	Hours
To:			Tot:		
Date:		End Time:		Bus	Charity
From:		Start Time:		Hours	Hours
To:			Tot:		
Date:		End Time:		Bus	Charity
From:		Start Time:		Hours	Hours
To:			Tot:		
Date:		End Time:		Bus	Charity
From:		Start Time:		Hours	Hours
To:			Tot:		
Date:		End Time:		Bus	Charity
From:		Start Time:		Hours	Hours
To:			Tot:		
Date:		End Time:		Bus	Charity
From:		Start Time:		Hours	Hours
To:			Tot:		
Date:		End Time:		Bus	Charity
From:		Start Time:		Hours	Hours
To:			Tot:		

March & Year to Date Summary of Hours			
	Business	Charity	Total
March:			
Feb YTD:			
YTD:			

DATE			TOTAL GALS	FUEL COST	QTS OIL		OIL COST
	Airfield	$/Gal			L	R	

MARCH EXPENSES

| March Fuel & Oil TOTALS: | | | | | | | |

| March Charity - Fuel & Oil Costs: | | | |

DATE	OTHER EXPENSES (Ramp, O_2, Oil change, etc.)	COST

FIXED EXPENSES	
Hangar	
Insurance	
Loan	

| GRAND TOTAL COST FOR March | |

FLIGHT HOURS / FUEL COST SUMMARY TO DATE				
	HOURS	GALS FUEL	FUEL COST	FUEL COST PER HR
March:				
+Feb YTD:				
YTD:				

VOR Check (every 30 days, FAR 91.171)		
Date & signature	Location & Method	Error or Bearing

GPS Database Updates (AIM 1-1-19)			
REV #	EFFECTIVE	EXPIRES	INSTALL DATE

Q 2
Monthly Flight Hours, Fuel and Oil Expenses, Oil Use Log, VOR Checks and GPS Database Updates

Q **2** *Oil Record*

Left Engine (or only engine) Oil Record			
Oil Changed @ Hrs:			
Oil Brand and Weight			
Next Oil Change Due:			
Qt(s) added	**Brand & Weight added**	**@ Tach / Hobbs**	**Engine Hrs per Qt**

Right Engine Oil Record			
Oil Changed @ Hrs:			
Oil Brand and Weight			
Next Oil Change Due:			
Qt(s) added	**Brand & Weight added**	**@ Tach / Hobbs**	**Engine Hrs per Qt**

April

Date:		End Time:		Bus Hours	Charity Hours
From:		Start Time:			
To:			Tot:		
Date:		End Time:		Bus Hours	Charity Hours
From:		Start Time:			
To:			Tot:		
Date:		End Time:		Bus Hours	Charity Hours
From:		Start Time:			
To:			Tot:		
Date:		End Time:		Bus Hours	Charity Hours
From:		Start Time:			
To:			Tot:		
Date:		End Time:		Bus Hours	Charity Hours
From:		Start Time:			
To:			Tot:		
Date:		End Time:		Bus Hours	Charity Hours
From:		Start Time:			
To:			Tot:		
Date:		End Time:		Bus Hours	Charity Hours
From:		Start Time:			
To:			Tot:		
Date:		End Time:		Bus Hours	Charity Hours
From:		Start Time:			
To:			Tot:		
Date:		End Time:		Bus Hours	Charity Hours
From:		Start Time:			
To:			Tot:		
Date:		End Time:		Bus Hours	Charity Hours
From:		Start Time:			
To:			Tot:		

April

Date:		End Time:		Bus Hours	Charity Hours
From:		Start Time:			
To:			Tot:		
Date:		End Time:		Bus Hours	Charity Hours
From:		Start Time:			
To:			Tot:		
Date:		End Time:		Bus Hours	Charity Hours
From:		Start Time:			
To:			Tot:		
Date:		End Time:		Bus Hours	Charity Hours
From:		Start Time:			
To:			Tot:		
Date:		End Time:		Bus Hours	Charity Hours
From:		Start Time:			
To:			Tot:		
Date:		End Time:		Bus Hours	Charity Hours
From:		Start Time:			
To:			Tot:		
Date:		End Time:		Bus Hours	Charity Hours
From:		Start Time:			
To:			Tot:		
Date:		End Time:		Bus Hours	Charity Hours
From:		Start Time:			
To:			Tot:		
Date:		End Time:		Bus Hours	Charity Hours
From:		Start Time:			
To:			Tot:		

April & Year to Date Summary of Hours			
	Business	Charity	Total
April:			
Mar YTD:			
YTD:			

DATE			TOTAL GALS	FUEL COST	QTS OIL		OIL COST
	Airfield	$/Gal			L	R	
April Fuel & Oil TOTALS:							
April Charity - Fuel & Oil Costs:							

APRIL EXPENSES

DATE	OTHER EXPENSES (Ramp, O$_2$, Oil change, etc.)	COST
FIXED EXPENSES		
	Hangar	
	Insurance	
	Loan	
GRAND TOTAL COST FOR April		

39

FLIGHT HOURS / FUEL COST SUMMARY TO DATE				
	HOURS	GALS FUEL	FUEL COST	FUEL COST PER HR
April:				
+Mar YTD:				
YTD:				

VOR Check (every 30 days, FAR 91.171)		
Date & signature	Location & Method	Error or Bearing

GPS Database Updates (AIM 1-1-19)			
REV #	EFFECTIVE	EXPIRES	INSTALL DATE

May

Date:		End Time:		Bus Hours	Charity Hours
From:		Start Time:			
To:			Tot:		
Date:		End Time:		Bus Hours	Charity Hours
From:		Start Time:			
To:			Tot:		
Date:		End Time:		Bus Hours	Charity Hours
From:		Start Time:			
To:			Tot:		
Date:		End Time:		Bus Hours	Charity Hours
From:		Start Time:			
To:			Tot:		
Date:		End Time:		Bus Hours	Charity Hours
From:		Start Time:			
To:			Tot:		
Date:		End Time:		Bus Hours	Charity Hours
From:		Start Time:			
To:			Tot:		
Date:		End Time:		Bus Hours	Charity Hours
From:		Start Time:			
To:			Tot:		
Date:		End Time:		Bus Hours	Charity Hours
From:		Start Time:			
To:			Tot:		
Date:		End Time:		Bus Hours	Charity Hours
From:		Start Time:			
To:			Tot:		
Date:		End Time:		Bus Hours	Charity Hours
From:		Start Time:			
To:			Tot:		

Date:		End Time:		Bus Hours	Charity Hours
From:		Start Time:			
To:			Tot:		
Date:		End Time:		Bus Hours	Charity Hours
From:		Start Time:			
To:			Tot:		
Date:		End Time:		Bus Hours	Charity Hours
From:		Start Time:			
To:			Tot:		
Date:		End Time:		Bus Hours	Charity Hours
From:		Start Time:			
To:			Tot:		
Date:		End Time:		Bus Hours	Charity Hours
From:		Start Time:			
To:			Tot:		
Date:		End Time:		Bus Hours	Charity Hours
From:		Start Time:			
To:			Tot:		
Date:		End Time:		Bus Hours	Charity Hours
From:		Start Time:			
To:			Tot:		
Date:		End Time:		Bus Hours	Charity Hours
From:		Start Time:			
To:			Tot:		
Date:		End Time:		Bus Hours	Charity Hours
From:		Start Time:			
To:			Tot:		

May & Year to Date Summary of Hours			
	Business	Charity	Total
May:			
April YTD:			
YTD:			

DATE			TOTAL GALS	FUEL COST	QTS OIL		OIL COST
	Airfield	$/Gal			L	R	

MAY EXPENSES

May Fuel & Oil TOTALS:						
May Charity - Fuel & Oil Costs:					

DATE	OTHER EXPENSES (Ramp, O₂, Oil change, etc.)	COST

FIXED EXPENSES	
Hangar	
Insurance	
Loan	

GRAND TOTAL COST FOR April	

FLIGHT HOURS / FUEL COST SUMMARY TO DATE				
	HOURS	GALS FUEL	FUEL COST	FUEL COST PER HR
May:				
+Apr YTD:				
YTD:				

VOR Check (every 30 days, FAR 91.171)		
Date & signature	Location & Method	Error or Bearing

GPS Database Updates (AIM 1-1-19)			
REV #	EFFECTIVE	EXPIRES	INSTALL DATE

June

Date:		End Time:		Bus Hours	Charity Hours
From:		Start Time:			
To:			Tot:		
Date:		End Time:		Bus Hours	Charity Hours
From:		Start Time:			
To:			Tot:		
Date:		End Time:		Bus Hours	Charity Hours
From:		Start Time:			
To:			Tot:		
Date:		End Time:		Bus Hours	Charity Hours
From:		Start Time:			
To:			Tot:		
Date:		End Time:		Bus Hours	Charity Hours
From:		Start Time:			
To:			Tot:		
Date:		End Time:		Bus Hours	Charity Hours
From:		Start Time:			
To:			Tot:		
Date:		End Time:		Bus Hours	Charity Hours
From:		Start Time:			
To:			Tot:		
Date:		End Time:		Bus Hours	Charity Hours
From:		Start Time:			
To:			Tot:		
Date:		End Time:		Bus Hours	Charity Hours
From:		Start Time:			
To:			Tot:		
Date:		End Time:		Bus Hours	Charity Hours
From:		Start Time:			
To:			Tot:		

June

Date:		End Time:		Bus Hours	Charity Hours
From:		Start Time:			
To:			Tot:		
Date:		End Time:		Bus Hours	Charity Hours
From:		Start Time:			
To:			Tot:		
Date:		End Time:		Bus Hours	Charity Hours
From:		Start Time:			
To:			Tot:		
Date:		End Time:		Bus Hours	Charity Hours
From:		Start Time:			
To:			Tot:		
Date:		End Time:		Bus Hours	Charity Hours
From:		Start Time:			
To:			Tot:		
Date:		End Time:		Bus Hours	Charity Hours
From:		Start Time:			
To:			Tot:		
Date:		End Time:		Bus Hours	Charity Hours
From:		Start Time:			
To:			Tot:		
Date:		End Time:		Bus Hours	Charity Hours
From:		Start Time:			
To:			Tot:		
Date:		End Time:		Bus Hours	Charity Hours
From:		Start Time:			
To:			Tot:		

June & Year to Date Summary of Hours			
	Business	Charity	Total
June:			
May YTD:			
YTD:			

46

DATE			TOTAL GALS	FUEL COST	QTS OIL		OIL COST
	Airfield	$/Gal			L	R	

JUNE EXPENSES

June Fuel & Oil TOTALS:					
June Charity - Fuel & Oil Costs:					

DATE	OTHER EXPENSES (Ramp, O_2, Oil change, etc.)	COST
	FIXED EXPENSES	
	Hangar	
	Insurance	
	Loan	
	GRAND TOTAL COST FOR June	

FLIGHT HOURS / FUEL COST SUMMARY TO DATE				
	HOURS	GALS FUEL	FUEL COST	FUEL COST PER HR
June:				
+May YTD:				
YTD:				

VOR Check (every 30 days, FAR 91.171)		
Date & signature	Location & Method	Error or Bearing

GPS Database Updates (AIM 1-1-19)			
REV #	EFFECTIVE	EXPIRES	INSTALL DATE

Q 3 Monthly Flight Hours, Fuel and Oil Expenses, Oil Use Log, VOR Checks and GPS Database Updates

Q 3 *Oil Record*

Left Engine (or only engine) Oil Record			
Oil Changed @ Hrs:			
Oil Brand and Weight			
Next Oil Change Due:			
Qt(s) added	**Brand & Weight added**	**@ Tach / Hobbs**	**Engine Hrs per Qt**

Right Engine Oil Record			
Oil Changed @ Hrs:			
Oil Brand and Weight			
Next Oil Change Due:			
Qt(s) added	**Brand & Weight added**	**@ Tach / Hobbs**	**Engine Hrs per Qt**

July

Date:		End Time:		Bus Hours	Charity Hours
From:		Start Time:			
To:			Tot:		
Date:		End Time:		Bus Hours	Charity Hours
From:		Start Time:			
To:			Tot:		
Date:		End Time:		Bus Hours	Charity Hours
From:		Start Time:			
To:			Tot:		
Date:		End Time:		Bus Hours	Charity Hours
From:		Start Time:			
To:			Tot:		
Date:		End Time:		Bus Hours	Charity Hours
From:		Start Time:			
To:			Tot:		
Date:		End Time:		Bus Hours	Charity Hours
From:		Start Time:			
To:			Tot:		
Date:		End Time:		Bus Hours	Charity Hours
From:		Start Time:			
To:			Tot:		
Date:		End Time:		Bus Hours	Charity Hours
From:		Start Time:			
To:			Tot:		
Date:		End Time:		Bus Hours	Charity Hours
From:		Start Time:			
To:			Tot:		
Date:		End Time:		Bus Hours	Charity Hours
From:		Start Time:			
To:			Tot:		

July

Date:		End Time:		Bus	Charity
From:		Start Time:		Hours	Hours
To:			Tot:		
Date:		End Time:		Bus	Charity
From:		Start Time:		Hours	Hours
To:			Tot:		
Date:		End Time:		Bus	Charity
From:		Start Time:		Hours	Hours
To:			Tot:		
Date:		End Time:		Bus	Charity
From:		Start Time:		Hours	Hours
To:			Tot:		
Date:		End Time:		Bus	Charity
From:		Start Time:		Hours	Hours
To:			Tot:		
Date:		End Time:		Bus	Charity
From:		Start Time:		Hours	Hours
To:			Tot:		
Date:		End Time:		Bus	Charity
From:		Start Time:		Hours	Hours
To:			Tot:		
Date:		End Time:		Bus	Charity
From:		Start Time:		Hours	Hours
To:			Tot:		
Date:		End Time:		Bus	Charity
From:		Start Time:		Hours	Hours
To:			Tot:		

July & Year to Date Summary of Hours

	Business	Charity	Total
July:			
June YTD:			
YTD:			

JULY EXPENSES

DATE	Airfield	$/Gal	TOTAL GALS	FUEL COST	QTS OIL L	QTS OIL R	OIL COST
July Fuel & Oil TOTALS:							
July Charity - Fuel & Oil Costs:							

DATE	OTHER EXPENSES (Ramp, O$_2$, Oil change, etc.)	COST
FIXED EXPENSES		
	Hangar	
	Insurance	
	Loan	
GRAND TOTAL COST FOR July		

FLIGHT HOURS / FUEL COST SUMMARY TO DATE				
	HOURS	GALS FUEL	FUEL COST	FUEL COST PER HR
July:				
+Jun YTD:				
YTD:				

VOR Check (every 30 days, FAR 91.171)		
Date & signature	Location & Method	Error or Bearing

GPS Database Updates (AIM 1-1-19)			
REV #	EFFECTIVE	EXPIRES	INSTALL DATE

August

Date:		End Time:		Bus Hours	Charity Hours
From:		Start Time:			
To:			Tot:		
Date:		End Time:		Bus Hours	Charity Hours
From:		Start Time:			
To:			Tot:		
Date:		End Time:		Bus Hours	Charity Hours
From:		Start Time:			
To:			Tot:		
Date:		End Time:		Bus Hours	Charity Hours
From:		Start Time:			
To:			Tot:		
Date:		End Time:		Bus Hours	Charity Hours
From:		Start Time:			
To:			Tot:		
Date:		End Time:		Bus Hours	Charity Hours
From:		Start Time:			
To:			Tot:		
Date:		End Time:		Bus Hours	Charity Hours
From:		Start Time:			
To:			Tot:		
Date:		End Time:		Bus Hours	Charity Hours
From:		Start Time:			
To:			Tot:		
Date:		End Time:		Bus Hours	Charity Hours
From:		Start Time:			
To:			Tot:		
Date:		End Time:		Bus Hours	Charity Hours
From:		Start Time:			
To:			Tot:		

August

Date:		End Time:		Bus Hours	Charity Hours
From:		Start Time:			
To:			Tot:		
Date:		End Time:		Bus Hours	Charity Hours
From:		Start Time:			
To:			Tot:		
Date:		End Time:		Bus Hours	Charity Hours
From:		Start Time:			
To:			Tot:		
Date:		End Time:		Bus Hours	Charity Hours
From:		Start Time:			
To:			Tot:		
Date:		End Time:		Bus Hours	Charity Hours
From:		Start Time:			
To:			Tot:		
Date:		End Time:		Bus Hours	Charity Hours
From:		Start Time:			
To:			Tot:		
Date:		End Time:		Bus Hours	Charity Hours
From:		Start Time:			
To:			Tot:		
Date:		End Time:		Bus Hours	Charity Hours
From:		Start Time:			
To:			Tot:		
Date:		End Time:		Bus Hours	Charity Hours
From:		Start Time:			
To:			Tot:		

August & Year to Date Summary of Hours			
	Business	Charity	Total
August:			
July YTD:			
YTD:			

DATE			TOTAL GALS	FUEL COST	QTS OIL		OIL COST
	Airfield	$/Gal			L	R	

AUGUST

August Fuel & Oil TOTALS:							

August Charity - Fuel & Oil Costs:	

DATE	OTHER EXPENSES (Ramp, O$_2$, Oil change, etc.)	COST

FIXED EXPENSES	
Hangar	
Insurance	
Loan	

GRAND TOTAL COST FOR August	

FLIGHT HOURS / FUEL COST SUMMARY TO DATE				
	HOURS	GALS FUEL	FUEL COST	FUEL COST PER HR
August:				
+Jul YTD:				
YTD:				

VOR Check (every 30 days, FAR 91.171)		
Date & signature	Location & Method	Error or Bearing

GPS Database Updates (AIM 1-1-19)			
REV #	EFFECTIVE	EXPIRES	INSTALL DATE

September

Date:		End Time:		Bus Hours	Charity Hours
From:		Start Time:			
To:			Tot:		
Date:		End Time:		Bus Hours	Charity Hours
From:		Start Time:			
To:			Tot:		
Date:		End Time:		Bus Hours	Charity Hours
From:		Start Time:			
To:			Tot:		
Date:		End Time:		Bus Hours	Charity Hours
From:		Start Time:			
To:			Tot:		
Date:		End Time:		Bus Hours	Charity Hours
From:		Start Time:			
To:			Tot:		
Date:		End Time:		Bus Hours	Charity Hours
From:		Start Time:			
To:			Tot:		
Date:		End Time:		Bus Hours	Charity Hours
From:		Start Time:			
To:			Tot:		
Date:		End Time:		Bus Hours	Charity Hours
From:		Start Time:			
To:			Tot:		
Date:		End Time:		Bus Hours	Charity Hours
From:		Start Time:			
To:			Tot:		
Date:		End Time:		Bus Hours	Charity Hours
From:		Start Time:			
To:			Tot:		

September

Date:		End Time:		Bus Hours	Charity Hours
From:		Start Time:			
To:			Tot:		
Date:		End Time:		Bus Hours	Charity Hours
From:		Start Time:			
To:			Tot:		
Date:		End Time:		Bus Hours	Charity Hours
From:		Start Time:			
To:			Tot:		
Date:		End Time:		Bus Hours	Charity Hours
From:		Start Time:			
To:			Tot:		
Date:		End Time:		Bus Hours	Charity Hours
From:		Start Time:			
To:			Tot:		
Date:		End Time:		Bus Hours	Charity Hours
From:		Start Time:			
To:			Tot:		
Date:		End Time:		Bus Hours	Charity Hours
From:		Start Time:			
To:			Tot:		
Date:		End Time:		Bus Hours	Charity Hours
From:		Start Time:			
To:			Tot:		
Date:		End Time:		Bus Hours	Charity Hours
From:		Start Time:			
To:			Tot:		

September & Year to Date Summary of Hours

	Business	Charity	Total
September:			
August YTD:			
YTD:			

DATE			TOTAL GALS	FUEL COST	QTS OIL		OIL COST
	Airfield	$/Gal			L	R	
Sept Fuel & Oil TOTALS:							
Sept Charity - Fuel & Oil Costs:							

SEPTEMBER EXPENSES

DATE	OTHER EXPENSES (Ramp, O$_2$, Oil change, etc.)	COST
FIXED EXPENSES		
	Hangar	
	Insurance	
	Loan	
GRAND TOTAL COST FOR September		

FLIGHT HOURS / FUEL COST SUMMARY TO DATE				
	HOURS	GALS FUEL	FUEL COST	FUEL COST PER HR
Sept:				
+Aug YTD:				
YTD:				

VOR Check (every 30 days, FAR 91.171)		
Date & signature	Location & Method	Error or Bearing

GPS Database Updates (AIM 1-1-19)			
REV #	EFFECTIVE	EXPIRES	INSTALL DATE

Q 4 Monthly Flight Hours, Fuel and Oil Expenses, Oil Use Log, VOR Checks and GPS Database Updates

Q4 *Oil Record*

Left Engine (or only engine) Oil Record			
Oil Changed @ Hrs:			
Oil Brand and Weight			
Next Oil Change Due:			
Qt(s) added	*Brand & Weight added*	*@ Tach / Hobbs*	*Engine Hrs per Qt*

Right Engine Oil Record			
Oil Changed @ Hrs:			
Oil Brand and Weight			
Next Oil Change Due:			
Qt(s) added	*Brand & Weight added*	*@ Tach / Hobbs*	*Engine Hrs per Qt*

October

Date:		End Time:		Bus Hours	Charity Hours
From:		Start Time:			
To:			Tot:		
Date:		End Time:		Bus Hours	Charity Hours
From:		Start Time:			
To:			Tot:		
Date:		End Time:		Bus Hours	Charity Hours
From:		Start Time:			
To:			Tot:		
Date:		End Time:		Bus Hours	Charity Hours
From:		Start Time:			
To:			Tot:		
Date:		End Time:		Bus Hours	Charity Hours
From:		Start Time:			
To:			Tot:		
Date:		End Time:		Bus Hours	Charity Hours
From:		Start Time:			
To:			Tot:		
Date:		End Time:		Bus Hours	Charity Hours
From:		Start Time:			
To:			Tot:		
Date:		End Time:		Bus Hours	Charity Hours
From:		Start Time:			
To:			Tot:		
Date:		End Time:		Bus Hours	Charity Hours
From:		Start Time:			
To:			Tot:		
Date:		End Time:		Bus Hours	Charity Hours
From:		Start Time:			
To:			Tot:		

Date:		End Time:		Bus	Charity
From:		Start Time:		Hours	Hours
To:			Tot:		
Date:		End Time:		Bus	Charity
From:		Start Time:		Hours	Hours
To:			Tot:		
Date:		End Time:		Bus	Charity
From:		Start Time:		Hours	Hours
To:			Tot:		
Date:		End Time:		Bus	Charity
From:		Start Time:		Hours	Hours
To:			Tot:		
Date:		End Time:		Bus	Charity
From:		Start Time:		Hours	Hours
To:			Tot:		
Date:		End Time:		Bus	Charity
From:		Start Time:		Hours	Hours
To:			Tot:		
Date:		End Time:		Bus	Charity
From:		Start Time:		Hours	Hours
To:			Tot:		
Date:		End Time:		Bus	Charity
From:		Start Time:		Hours	Hours
To:			Tot:		
Date:		End Time:		Bus	Charity
From:		Start Time:		Hours	Hours
To:			Tot:		

October & Year to Date Summary of Hours			
	Business	Charity	Total
October:			
Sep YTD:			
YTD:			

DATE			TOTAL GALS	FUEL COST	QTS OIL		OIL COST
	Airfield	$/Gal			L	R	
October Fuel & Oil TOTALS:							
October Charity - Fuel & Oil Costs:							

OCTOBER EXPENSES

DATE	OTHER EXPENSES (Ramp, O$_2$, Oil change, etc.)	COST
FIXED EXPENSES		
	Hangar	
	Insurance	
	Loan	
GRAND TOTAL COST FOR October		

FLIGHT HOURS / FUEL COST SUMMARY TO DATE				
	HOURS	**GALS FUEL**	**FUEL COST**	**FUEL COST PER HR**
Oct:				
+Sep YTD:				
YTD:				

VOR Check **(every 30 days,** FAR 91.171**)**		
Date & signature	Location & Method	Error or Bearing

GPS Database Updates (AIM 1-1-19)			
REV #	EFFECTIVE	EXPIRES	INSTALL DATE

November

Date:		End Time:		Bus Hours	Charity Hours
From:		Start Time:			
To:			Tot:		
Date:		End Time:		Bus Hours	Charity Hours
From:		Start Time:			
To:			Tot:		
Date:		End Time:		Bus Hours	Charity Hours
From:		Start Time:			
To:			Tot:		
Date:		End Time:		Bus Hours	Charity Hours
From:		Start Time:			
To:			Tot:		
Date:		End Time:		Bus Hours	Charity Hours
From:		Start Time:			
To:			Tot:		
Date:		End Time:		Bus Hours	Charity Hours
From:		Start Time:			
To:			Tot:		
Date:		End Time:		Bus Hours	Charity Hours
From:		Start Time:			
To:			Tot:		
Date:		End Time:		Bus Hours	Charity Hours
From:		Start Time:			
To:			Tot:		
Date:		End Time:		Bus Hours	Charity Hours
From:		Start Time:			
To:			Tot:		
Date:		End Time:		Bus Hours	Charity Hours
From:		Start Time:			
To:			Tot:		

November

Date:		End Time:		Bus	Charity
From:		Start Time:		Hours	Hours
To:			Tot:		
Date:		End Time:		Bus	Charity
From:		Start Time:		Hours	Hours
To:			Tot:		
Date:		End Time:		Bus	Charity
From:		Start Time:		Hours	Hours
To:			Tot:		
Date:		End Time:		Bus	Charity
From:		Start Time:		Hours	Hours
To:			Tot:		
Date:		End Time:		Bus	Charity
From:		Start Time:		Hours	Hours
To:			Tot:		
Date:		End Time:		Bus	Charity
From:		Start Time:		Hours	Hours
To:			Tot:		
Date:		End Time:		Bus	Charity
From:		Start Time:		Hours	Hours
To:			Tot:		
Date:		End Time:		Bus	Charity
From:		Start Time:		Hours	Hours
To:			Tot:		
Date:		End Time:		Bus	Charity
From:		Start Time:		Hours	Hours
To:			Tot:		

November & Year to Date Summary of Hours			
	Business	Charity	Total
November:			
Oct YTD:			
YTD:			

DATE			TOTAL GALS	FUEL COST	QTS OIL		OIL COST
	Airfield	$/Gal			L	R	

NOVEMBER EXPENSES

November Fuel & Oil TOTALS:					
November Charity - Fuel & Oil Costs:					

DATE	OTHER EXPENSES (Ramp, O$_2$, Oil change, etc.)	COST
	FIXED EXPENSES	
	Hangar	
	Insurance	
	Loan	
	GRAND TOTAL COST FOR November	

FLIGHT HOURS / FUEL COST SUMMARY TO DATE				
	HOURS	GALS FUEL	FUEL COST	FUEL COST PER HR
Nov:				
+Oct YTD:				
YTD:				

VOR Check (every 30 days, FAR 91.171)		
Date & signature	Location & Method	Error or Bearing

GPS Database Updates (AIM 1-1-19)			
REV #	EFFECTIVE	EXPIRES	INSTALL DATE

December

Date:		End Time:		Bus Hours	Charity Hours
From:		Start Time:			
To:			Tot:		
Date:		End Time:		Bus Hours	Charity Hours
From:		Start Time:			
To:			Tot:		
Date:		End Time:		Bus Hours	Charity Hours
From:		Start Time:			
To:			Tot:		
Date:		End Time:		Bus Hours	Charity Hours
From:		Start Time:			
To:			Tot:		
Date:		End Time:		Bus Hours	Charity Hours
From:		Start Time:			
To:			Tot:		
Date:		End Time:		Bus Hours	Charity Hours
From:		Start Time:			
To:			Tot:		
Date:		End Time:		Bus Hours	Charity Hours
From:		Start Time:			
To:			Tot:		
Date:		End Time:		Bus Hours	Charity Hours
From:		Start Time:			
To:			Tot:		
Date:		End Time:		Bus Hours	Charity Hours
From:		Start Time:			
To:			Tot:		
Date:		End Time:		Bus Hours	Charity Hours
From:		Start Time:			
To:			Tot:		

December

Date:		End Time:		Bus	Charity
From:		Start Time:		Hours	Hours
To:			Tot:		
Date:		End Time:		Bus	Charity
From:		Start Time:		Hours	Hours
To:			Tot:		
Date:		End Time:		Bus	Charity
From:		Start Time:		Hours	Hours
To:			Tot:		
Date:		End Time:		Bus	Charity
From:		Start Time:		Hours	Hours
To:			Tot:		
Date:		End Time:		Bus	Charity
From:		Start Time:		Hours	Hours
To:			Tot:		
Date:		End Time:		Bus	Charity
From:		Start Time:		Hours	Hours
To:			Tot:		
Date:		End Time:		Bus	Charity
From:		Start Time:		Hours	Hours
To:			Tot:		
Date:		End Time:		Bus	Charity
From:		Start Time:		Hours	Hours
To:			Tot:		
Date:		End Time:		Bus	Charity
From:		Start Time:		Hours	Hours
To:			Tot:		

December & Year to Date Summary of Hours			
	Business	Charity	Total
December:			
Nov YTD:			
YTD:			

DATE			TOTAL	FUEL	QTS OIL		OIL
	Airfield	$/Gal	GALS	COST	L	R	COST

DECEMBER EXPENSES

December Fuel & Oil TOTALS:					
December Charity - Fuel & Oil Costs:					

DATE	OTHER EXPENSES (Ramp, O₂, Oil change, etc.)	COST

FIXED EXPENSES	
Hangar	
Insurance	
Loan	
GRAND TOTAL COST FOR December	

75

FLIGHT HOURS / FUEL COST SUMMARY TO DATE				
	HOURS	GALS FUEL	FUEL COST	FUEL COST PER HR
Dec:				
+Nov YTD:				
YTD:				

VOR Check (every 30 days, FAR 91.171)		
Date & signature	Location & Method	Error or Bearing

GPS Database Updates (AIM 1-1-19)			
REV #	EFFECTIVE	EXPIRES	INSTALL DATE

Monthly and End of Year Costs/Tax Summary

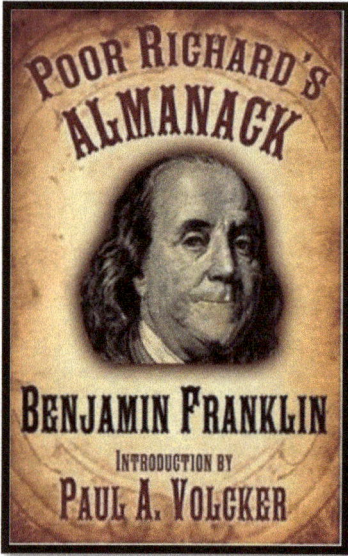

"It would be a hard government that should tax its people one-tenth part of their income."

~ Benjamin Franklin, Poor Richard's Almanac

"The difference between death and taxes is death doesn't get worse every time Congress meets."

~ Will Rogers

MONTHLY COST SUMMARY

	Fuel	Oil	Ramp	O2	Other	Hangar	Ins	Loan
Jan								
Feb								
Mar								
Apr								
May								
Jun								
Jul								
Aug								
Sep								
Oct								
Nov								
Dec								
TOT								

MONTHLY SUMMARY: Total Hours, Business Hours/Percentage + Charity Fuel and Oil Costs

	Business Hrs	Total Hours	Charity Fuel Cost	Charity Oil Cost
Jan				
Feb				
Mar				
Apr				
May				
Jun				
Jul				
Aug				
Sep				
Oct				
Nov				
Dec				
TOTAL				
Business % OF TOTAL HRS:			**CHARITY TOTAL Fuel and Oil Cost:**	

CALCULATING MX RESERVES
Hourly Costs (HOBBS/TACH)

	Replacement or Overhaul Cost	Hours of Service Life	Cost Per Hour	Actual Hours this Year	Hourly Reserve Cost this Year
Engine		/	=	X	=
Vacuum Pump(s)		/	=	X	=
Prop(s)*		/	=	X	=
Total hourly RESERVE costs this year:					

Yearly Service Life Costs (CALENDAR)

	Replacement, Overhaul or Upgrade Cost	Years of Service Life	Service Life Cost this Year
Prop(s)*		/	=
Paint		/	=
Interior		/	=
Avionics		/	=
Total Service Life RESERVE Costs this Year:			
Total Hourly and Service Life RESERVE Costs this Year:			

*Some prop manufacturers base the time top overhaul on hours or months, whichever occurs first. Therefore, a *Prop(s)* column appears in matrixes for both *"Hourly Costs" and "Yearly Service Life Costs"*; your choice.

The Year's OIL USAGE

TOTAL TACH/HOBBS HOURS	TOTAL OIL ADDED	TOTAL OIL ADDED LEFT	TOTAL OIL ADDED RIGHT

Hours flown per quart – LEFT:	
Hours flown per quart – RIGHT:	
Hours flown per quart – TOTAL:	

The Year's FUEL SUMMARY

TOTAL FUEL USED	TOTAL FUEL COSTS	AVERAGE FUEL COST PER GALLON

80

END OF CALENDAR and TAX SUMMARY

20___	Cost			
Fuel				
Oil				
Ramp				
Other				
O2				
Hanger				
Insurance		Charity Fuel and Oil Tax Deduction		
Loan				
Reserves				
Maintenance and Navigation COSTS			Total	
TOTAL COST		x	**Business hr %**	

(Business Tax Deduction)

Worried about an IRS audit? Avoid what's called a red flag. That's something the IRS always looks for. For example, say you have some money left in your bank account after taxes. That's a red flag." ~ Jay Leno

Try to learn from the mistakes of others.
You won't live long enough to make all of them by yourself

BONUS
Section

Flight Regulations

Preparation Prior to Each Flight
(FAR 91.103)

If you plan to fly outside of the airport area, or file IFR, you must:

- o Study weather reports and forecasts.
- o Determine fuel requirements.
- o Plan alternatives if the planned flight cannot be completed.
- o Check with ATC for known traffic delays.
- o Determine takeoff and landing distances by evaluating:
  - • Runway lengths, elevation and slope.
  - • Aircraft gross weight.
  - • Wind and temperature.

For Local Flights: You should know about the airport(s) you intend to use. This includes the runway lengths, and takeoff and landing distances for the conditions of the day.

Planning Fuel Requirements
(FAR 91.151 & 167)

- o **VFR DAY:** Fuel to destination + 30 minutes.
- o **VFR NIGHT:** Fuel to destination + 45 minutes.
- o **IFR:** Fuel to destination and alternate + 45 minutes.

"Any attempt to stretch fuel is guaranteed to increase headwinds."

According to AOPA's Air Safety Institute, in an average week, three general aviation aircraft crash due to improper fuel management.

Your Responsibility and Authority as the Pilot in Command (PIC) *(FAR 91.3)*

You are directly responsible for, and are the final authority as to the operation of the aircraft.

Deviating From the Rules *(FAR 91.3)*

- o If an in-flight emergency requires immediate action, the PIC may deviate from any rule necessary to deal with that emergency.
- o If the PIC deviates from a rule, he or she shall, upon the request of the Administrator, send a written report of that deviation to the Administrator.

PIC Responsibilities *(FAR 91.413)*

The PIC must make sure that his/her aircraft is airworthy. That includes ensuring that:

- o The aircraft has received an Annual Inspection within the past 12 months. (The annual expires the last day of the 12th month). (FAR 91.409).
- o The transponder has been tested and inspected within the past 24 months. (Expires the last day of the 24th month).

If you're flying IFR, the Pitot/Static System must have been tested and inspected within the past 24 months. (Expires the last day of the 24th month).

Pilot Preventive Maintenance *(CFR Part 43, Maintenance, Preventative Maintenance, Rebuilding & Alteration)*

Pilots should never exceed their personal skill level when it comes to aircraft maintenance.

A pilot can:

- o Change the oil and lubricate the wheel bearings.
- o Refill the hydraulic fluid.
- o Remove, install, and repair landing gear tires.
- o Replace the landing gear's elastic shock absorber cords.
- o Replace defective safety wiring and cotter keys.
- o Lubricate cover plates, cowlings, and fairings
- o Add oil or air to landing gear shock struts.

Required Documents in the Aircraft
(FAR 91.203, 91.9)

- o **A**irworthiness certificate.

- o **R**egistration certificate.

- o **R**adio license, (if traveling outside the USA, and for some commercial operations).

- o **O**perating limitations - - (The Owner's Manual).

- o **W**eight and balance data.

Medicals (FAR 61.23)

- o 3rd Class — Good for 60 months, unless you're 40 or over on the day of the examination; then it's good for 24 months.
- o 2nd Class — Good for Commercial privileges the first 12 months. If you don't get another flight physical after 12 months — it turns into a 3rd class physical.
- o 1st Class — ATP privileges during first 6 months, Commercial privileges during the next 6 months. After 12 months — it turns into a 3rd class physical.

There are certain aircraft sounds that can only be heard at night or over large bodies of water.

Flight Physical Expiration Table

(ALL PHYSICALS expire the last day of the month.)

Flight Purpose:	3rd Class	2nd Class		1st Class		
	Personal & Business	Comm-ercial	Personal & Business (3rd Class)	ATP (1st Class)	Comm-ercial	Personal & Business (3rd Class)
If you are under 40	60 months	12 months	60 months	12 months	12 months	60 months
If you are 40 or older	24 months	12 months	24 months	6 months	12 months	24 months

REMEMBER, you can submit FAA Form 8500-8 before your physical at:
https://medxpress.faa.gov
The FAA forwards this information to your Medical Examiner.

Pilot Currency *(FAR 61.56, 61.57)*

Within the preceding 24 calendar months you must have received a Flight Review in **one** of the aircraft in which you're rated.

Landing Currency is Category, Class and Type specific.

*If you'll be carrying passengers **in a particular aircraft**, you'll need, within the past 90 days:*

- o **DAY CURRENCY: Three** takeoffs and landings. (If it's a tail wheel aircraft, those landings need to be to a full stop).
- o **NIGHT CURRENCY**: From one hour after sunset to one hour before sunrise, **three** takeoffs and **three** landings to a **full stop**.

Required Personal Documents *(FAR 61.3)*

When you are flying, you must have with you:

- o A current plastic (credit card style) pilot certificate that includes an "English Proficient" endorsement. (Required for international flying).
- o An appropriate current medical.
- o A photo ID (Driver's license, government ID, military ID, or passport).

Misplaced License

You can request temporary authority to exercise certificate privileges from *www.FAA.gov*. Go to FAA.gov and sign into your account, and click on *Licenses & Certificates*. Next, click on *Airman Online Services*. FAA will send a temporary certificate via fax or e-mail. You can only request one temporary certificate within any six-month period.
While you're there, you can request your **replacement** certificate.

Changed Address and Your Certificate
(FAR 61.60)

The FAA must be notified within **30 days** of an address change, otherwise you may not act as pilot in command. You can change your address, add "English Proficient", or any other amendment to your status by going to *www.FAA.gov, and clicking* on the "Licenses & Certificates" TAB.

You may also make changes through the mail, at:
FAA
Airmen Certification Branch,
AFS-760
P.O. Box 25082
Oklahoma City, OK 73125-0082

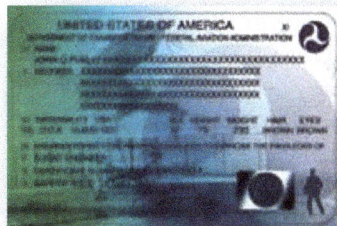

Required Equipment, VFR

DAY:

o Fuel gauge for each tank.
o Oil Temp gauge, (each air cooled engine).
o Oil Pressure gauge, (each engine).
o Temp gauge, (each liquid cooled engine).
o ELT (FAR 91.207).
o Altimeter.
o Magnetic Compass.
o Airspeed Indicator.
o Tachometer, (each engine).
o Manifold Pressure gauge, for each altitude engine.
(An altitude engine is a turbocharged reciprocating engine. Its manifold pressure is boosted and therefore, one must monitor that pressure).
o Landing gear position indicator, (if the aircraft has retractable gear).
o Anti-collision light system, if certified after March 11, 1996.
   • In the event of failure, you may continue to a location where repairs or replacement can be made.
o Seat Belts and shoulder straps, if installed. (Installed shoulder straps are mandatory if the aircraft was manufactured after July, 1978).
o Seat belts and shoulder straps, (if installed), are required during taxi, takeoff and landing. (FAR 91.107).
o If a child is less than 24 months old, he or she can be held on a passenger's lap.

NIGHT:

o Anti-collision light system, if certified after August 11, 1971.
   • In the event of failure, you may continue to a location where repairs or replacement can be made.
o Position lights must be ON from sunset to sunrise. (Ref. FAR 91.209).
o Landing light, (if flown for hire).
o A power source.
o Spare fuses; 3 of each kind required, and accessible in flight.

Required Equipment for an IFR Flight
(In addition to the equipment required for VFR) (FAR 91.205)
- o   Clock installed in the aircraft, displaying hours, minutes and seconds.
- o   Directional Gyro (DG).
- o   Attitude Indicator.
- o   Rate of turn indicator or an additional attitude indicator
- o   Skid/Slip Indicator.
- o   Two-way radios and NAV equipment appropriate to the ground facilities to be used.
- o   Altimeter.
- o   Generator or Alternator with adequate capacity.

You can take off with inoperative instruments or equipment that are not required by FAR 91, as long as the "bad" instrument or equipment is removed or placarded "INOPERATIVE", and a pilot or mechanic determines that the loss of that instrument or equipment is not a hazard.

Minimum Equipment List (MEL) (FAR 91.213)
A **MEL** can be authorized by the airworthiness certificate holder to allow take off with inoperative instruments or equipment. It can never take away from the equipment required for VFR day, VFR night, or IFR (day or night).
- o   The MEL must be approved by the FAA.
- o   The MEL and the FAA's letter of approval must be carried in the aircraft.

Stations, Seatbelts, and Shoulder Harnesses
(FAR 91.107)
As pilot in command, you'll need to ensure that each passenger has been:
- o   Briefed on how to fasten and unfasten their safety belt, and if applicable, their shoulder harness*.
- o   Notified to fasten his/her safety belt/shoulder harness* before aircraft movement.
- o   Passengers must be in an appropriate seat** with their safety belt/shoulder harness fastened during taxi, takeoff and landing.

*Shoulder straps must be installed if the aircraft was manufactured after July, 1978.
**If a child is less than 24 months old, he or she can be held on a passenger's lap. See FAR 91.107 for child approved seat/restraint systems.

Minimum Safe Altitudes *(FAR 91.119)*

Anywhere – Fly at an altitude that will allow a safe emergency landing without hazard to people or property on the surface.

1,000'

Congested Areas: Fly no closer than **1,000 feet** above the highest obstacle within **2,000 feet** of the aircraft.

500'

Other than congested areas and over water and sparsely populated areas: Fly no closer than **500 feet** to any person, vessel, vehicle or structure.

Acrobatic Flight *(FAR 91.303)*

You cannot perform acrobatics:

- o Over a congested area or settlement.
- o Over an open air assembly.
- o Within Class B, C, D, or Class E <u>if it's designated for an airport.</u>
- o Within 4 nm of a federal airway (Class E).
- o Below 1,500 feet AGL.
- o When visibility is less than 3 statute miles.

Acrobatic Flight Defined

Acrobatic flight means an intentional maneuver involving an abrupt change in the aircraft's attitude, an abnormal attitude, or abnormal acceleration that is not necessary for flight. It also means:

- o Exceeding 60° of bank.
- o Exceeding 30° pitch – nose up or nose down.

Acrobatic Flight and Parachutes *(FAR 91.307)*

Unless each occupant is wearing a parachute, no pilot carrying any person (other than a crew member) may execute acrobatic maneuvers.

This does not apply to spins or other flight maneuvers required by the regulations for a certificate or rating, when given by a CFI, etc.

Formation Flying *(FAR 91.111)*

It's never done:

- ○ Without prior arrangement with the pilots of all aircraft involved.
- ○ If carrying passengers for hire.

Cruising Altitudes *(FAR 91.179)*

GREATER THAN 3,000 FEET AGL, BUT LESS THEN 18,000 FEET MSL, FLY:

Choosing an appropriate altitude is based on magnetic degrees <u>track</u>, not magnetic degrees heading.

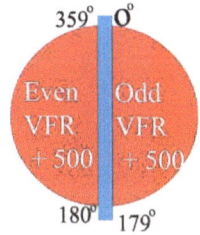

359° 0°

Even VFR + 500   Odd VFR + 500

180° 179°

Order of Right of Way *(FAR 91.113)*

BALLOON has the right of way over everything.

GLIDER — It's the next least Maneuverable and has the right of way over an airplane or a rotorcraft.

AIRCRAFT TOWING OR REFUELING another aircraft has the right of way over all other engine driven aircraft.

AIRCRAFT IN DISTRESS have the right-of-way over <u>all</u> other aircraft.

Converging, Approaching Head-On, and Overtaking *(FAR 91.111)*

- o **IF CONVERGING** — an aircraft on the right has the right of way, (if it's the same category aircraft).
- o **IF APPROACHING HEAD-ON** — **both aircraft** should alter course to the right.
- o **IF OVERTAKING** — the overtaken aircraft has the right of way. The pilot of the **overtaking aircraft** alters course to the right.

Right of Way While Landing *(FAR 91.113)*
Final approach or landing aircraft have the right of way.

- o If you're at a lower altitude, you have the right of way, but you should never take advantage of your position.

Oxygen *(FAR 91.211)*

ABOVE 15,000 MSL:	Oxygen available for everyone.
ABOVE 14,000 MSL:	Oxygen is required for flight crew at all times.
14,000 MSL ⇕ 12,500 MSL	Oxygen is required for flight crew after 30 minutes.

Supplemental oxygen can help prevent hypoxia symptoms when flying:

- o *At or above 5,000 feet MSL at night.*
- o *At or above 10,000 feet MSL during the day*

ELTs

An ELT must be attached to the airplane and the ELT batteries must be checked annually for corrosion. *The ELT batteries must be replaced:*

1. If the transmitter has been in use for more than 1 cumulative hour,

    or

2. When either 50% of their useful life, *or* 50% of their charge life has expired.

406 MHz ELTs

On **February 1, 2009,** the international COSPAS-SARSAT satellite system discontinued satellite-based monitoring of the 121.5 and 243 MHz frequencies.

121.5 / 243 MHz distress signals are now, only detected by local airport facilities, air traffic control facilities, or by overflying aircraft. This assumes that an overflying aircraft will be monitoring 121.5. If an aircraft crashes, especially in a remote area, a **121.5 MHz ELT** will provide extremely limited assistance.

The new **406 MHz ELTs** are monitored by satellites and also contain a 121.5 MHZ ELT. Optionally, they can be linked to a GPS, to provide precise coordinates to search responders.
If you don't have a 406 ELT, consider carrying a personal locator beacon, (PLB).

It's your choice. Base your decision on the type of flying you do, the equipment you carry, and the type of terrain you overfly.

Drugs and Alcohol *(FAR 91.17)*

You cannot be a crew member if:

- You're using any drug that affects your physical or mental capacities in any way.
- You've consumed alcohol within eight hours.
  - You could be under the influence after 8 hours. Therefore, you would be wise to allow **12 to 24** hours from bottle to throttle.

You're under the influence if your blood alcohol **is .04% or more**.

Passengers & Substance Abuse

If your passenger(s) cannot correctly pronounce "innovative", "preliminary", "proliferation", or "cinnamon" – they may be under the influence. So, except in an emergency, a pilot may not allow anyone to board his/her aircraft if they appear to be intoxicated or under the influence of drugs. The exception is a medical patient under proper care.

Consider This:

Drunk passengers aboard a short charter flight near Canada's West Coast, likely caused the crash of a float-equipped Cessna 185 in May 2010. A rear-seat passenger pushed the pilot's seat forward with his or her feet and held him and the control column pinned to the panel. The chartered aircraft dove at a 45° angle into the ocean off Ahousat, an isolated community on the west coast of Vancouver Island. The pilot could have refused the charter if he thought the passengers might be drunk enough to be a safety hazard. This decision cost him his life.

Refusing to Submit to a Drug or Alcohol Test *(FAR 61.14)*

That's grounds for denying an application for any certificate or rating for a year, and suspension or revocation of any certificate or rating.

Carbon Monoxide is a big concern, especially in the winter. Most heaters work by air flowing over the manifold. If exhaust fumes escape, the results could be fatal. If you detect the odor of exhaust or feel drowsy, dizzy, or have a headache while using the heater, you should suspect carbon monoxide poisoning.

Inflight Weather Resources

Automated Weather Observing Systems (AWOS) & Automated Weather Surface Observing Systems (ASOS) facts:

- o If broadcast on a VOR frequency, it is designated by an "A" in the NAVAID's frequency box.
- o Otherwise, its frequency is listed on the chart near the airport data.
  - **AWOS-A:** Simply reports the altimeter setting.
  - **AWOS-1:** Reports altimeter setting, wind data, temperature/dew point, and density altitude, (when it exceeds the field elevation by more than 1,000 feet).
  - **AWOS-2:** Like AWOS-1, plus visibility.
  - **AWOS-3:** Like AWOS-2, plus cloud/ceiling data, (below 12,000 feet AGL).
  - **ASOS:** Like AWOS-3, plus precipitation.

When checking in with an approach controller for landing at an airport with ASOS or AWOS, simply include that you have the landing airport's "one minute weather".

En-route Flight Advisory Service (EFAS), or "Flight Watch" — EFAS can provide weather

updates, PIREPs, and advisories. Call them on 122.0 (below 18,000 feet MSL). Use the ATC facility's name, "Los Angeles Flight Watch", not the Flight Service name. *EFAS is available:*

- o Above 5,000 AGL to 17,500 MSL.
- o 7 days a week, 6 am to 10 pm local.

In many areas, it's possible to make contact well below 5,000' AGL. Give it a try before you start a climb.

Providing a PIREP to EFAS, 122.0

The Required Stuff, PIREP:

- o **LOCATION** (Nearest VOR or Airport).
- o **TIME**—ZULU or minutes ago.
- o **ALTITUDE** (MSL).
- o **A/C TYPE.**

Optional Stuff, PIREP:

- o **CLOUD COVERAGE** - (CLR, FEW, SCT, BKN, OVC), **TYPE** - (Cirrus, Cumulus, Stratus), & **HEIGHT** - (Bases & Tops should be expressed in feet MSL).
- o **VISIBILITY** - (in statute miles), & **RESTRICTIONS** - (Haze, Mist, Fog, Dust, Sand, Smoke, Spray, Volcanic Ash).
- o **PRECIP TYPE** - (Rain, drizzle, snow, and hail), & **INTENSITY** - (Light, moderate, or heavy).
- o **TEMP** - (Celsius).
- o **WIND** - (Direction & Speed in knots)
- o **TURBULENCE** - (Light, light chop, moderate, moderate chop, severe, or extreme).
- o **ICING** - (Trace, light, moderate, or severe).
- o **REMARKS.**

AOPA's online PIREP course, "*Sky Spotter*" and several of their Aviation Weather courses – "*Weather Wise*", are available at **AOPA.org**.

Transcribed Weather En route Broadcast (TWEB)
TWEBs are becoming rare, but if you find one:

- They are recorded on tape, and broadcast on selected VOR frequencies.
- They are designated by a "T" in the NAVAID's frequency box.
- They are issued 3 times each day, providing sky cover, visibility, winds, & NOTAMS.
- Up to five reporting station's weather observations can be included in a TWEB.

Hazardous In-flight Weather Advisory Service (HIWAS)

- Available on select VOR frequencies.
- Designated by a circled "H" in the NAVAID's frequency box.

In areas serviced by HIWAS, centers (ARTCC), tower facilities and flight service stations will not broadcast in-flight weather advisories. They will, however, broadcast that an advisory has been published, and tell you to tune in to HIWAS for details.

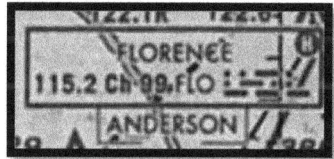

Calling Flight Service (Radio)
By Debby Colvin, Lockheed Martin Quality Assurance Specialist.

To ensure a quick radio response from flight service, here are some suggestions:

- On the initial call, always give the frequency and your current location using NAVAIDs or airport references with your request.
- Always use your full aircraft identification on initial call-up.

If you are unsure of the name of your nearest flight service station, provide the geographical area of your position. Rather than broadcasting for "Any Radio, N12345," you should transmit, "Radio near Greenwood, Mississippi, N12345."

Flight Planning

Flight Service Resources

The briefer will need to know the following:

1) VFR or IFR.

2) Registration Number.

3) Aircraft Type.

4) Departure airport's ID.

5) Departure time (ZULU).

6) Altitude.

7) Route.

8) Destination airport's ID.

9) Time en route.

Ask the briefer, "Are there any Temporary Flight Restrictions (TFRs)?" (This puts it on tape).

IFR Clearance Delivery: 888 SPOT-BOT (766-8267)	Flight Service Problems? 888-FLT-SRVC (358-7782)

Flight Service Briefing Types

An Outlook Briefing is a synopsis. Its forecast range is more than 6 hours out and up to 5 days ahead.

Standard (6 Hours or Less from Take off)

- o Current and forecast weather.
- o Adverse conditions.
- o Winds aloft.
- o NOTAMS & TFRs.
- o "VFR not recommended".

Abbreviated

This updates a previously received Standard briefing.

You must ask for specific:

- o Weather forecasts.
- o NOTAMS.
- o TFRs.

TIBS (Telephone Information Briefing Service)

Call Flt Svc (800-WX-BRIEF), then press "3" or say "TIBS." Also, TIBS line: 877-4TIBS-WX. Includes SIGMETs, AIRMETs METARs, TAFs, winds aloft. (This recording does not constitute a weather briefing).

Lockheed Martin Tips, Reference www.afss.com

"Early morning hours, 06:00-10:00, are our busiest times. If your schedule permits, call before or after this time.
File your flight plan with flight service during off hours, well in advance of your scheduled departure. (If you plan to depart at 07:00 local time, file your flight plan the night before)."

AOPA's online course, "*A Pilot's Guide to Flight Service*", is available at **AOPA.org**.

FAA Authorized Internet Briefing Sites

The FAA has authorized two replacements for the telephone weather briefing:

www.*DUAT.COM*. Full weather brief and NOTAMS – files your flight plans - FREE

Also see ***DUAT.com/mobile***

DTC Duat's SmartPhone app

www.*DUATS.com*

Full weather brief and NOTAMS - files flight plans — FREE.

Internet Flight Planning Tools

Also see ***Aeroplanner.com/MOBILE*** *(Mobile requires a Premium membership)*.

Flight Planning, File flight plans - IFR & VFR (uses DUATS), Weather, NOTAMS, Airport Directory/Lodging, Approach Charts, and Logbook.

AOPA.org (AOPA membership required)

Flight Planning, file flight plans, weather, NOTAMS, Airport Directory, Approach Charts. ***AOPA Airports SmartPhone app***.

FREE. Also see *FltPlan.com/PDA* — FREE Flight Planning, file IFR flight plans, check previous clearances for the same route, checks RAIM (IFR flights).

After you file, you can read your actual ATC clearance. Weather, NOTAMS, Airport Directory, Approach Charts. Flight tracking, tell the FBO that you're coming, and more. *FltPlan Mobile* and **FltPlan.com FltDeck Airport/FBO Guide** SmartPhone/iPad apps.
FltPlan.com is an FAA approved and certified source of Weather and Notams. It is a QICP (Qualified Internet Communications Provider) weather service.

FREE. Fuel Prices / Plan a trip with either the cheapest or quickest fuel stops

Airport Information + NAVAIDs & fixes. Lodging, and AIRBOSS fuel program.
AirNav FBO iPhone app – small annual fee, but FREE to AirBoss® members.

Maps.AvnWx.com

AvnWx.com
Aviation Weather

FREE. TFRs, SIGMETS, AIRMETS, winds, route briefing, NEXRAD radar, METAR/TAF/PIREPS, temps aloft, NOTAMS, airport details, & A/FD.

NOAA

www.aviationweather.gov/adds/

FREE
Every weather tool you can imagine, including those using powerful JAVA programs.

ForeFlight **iPhone and iPad** app – *does everything. Includes GPS flight following on charts.*

Aircraft Loading

Aft Center of Gravity (CG) Characteristics

- Less wing loading = a slower stall speed.
- Reduced drag. A smaller angle of attack is required to maintain level flight, so the cruise speed is higher.
- Less stable & less controllable.

IF THE CG IS AFT OF THE AIRCRAFT'S AFT CG LIMIT:

The aircraft could stall after takeoff or Go-Around. (Not enough elevator authority to recover).

RULES AND LAWS
Rules are made by those who are trying to keep you safe. Laws of Physics are set by the Almighty. You may find it necessary to suspend a Rule, but you can never suspend a Law.

Forward Center of Gravity (CG) Characteristics

- Increased wing loading = a higher stall speed.
- Increased drag and a greater angle of attack to maintain level flight, so the cruise speed is slower.
- More stable & controllable.

IF THE CG IS FORWARD OF THE AIRCRAFT'S FORWARD CG LIMIT:

- It's harder to rotate, and flare.
- Takeoff rolls are longer.

Calculating
Weight & Moment

FORMULA: **WT X ARM = MOMENT**			
	Weight	**x ARM**	**= Moment**
Airplane's Basic Empty Weight			
Pilot			
Front seat Passenger			
Rear seat Passenger(s)			
Fuel _____ gal.			
Cargo			

Total moment, divided by total weight, equals the CG

Total Moment	/ Total Weight	= CG

WEIGHTS	
AvGas	**6 lb / gal**
Jet A	**6.75 lb / gal**
Oil	**1.9 lb / qt**
Water	**8.3 lb / gal**

Takeoff and Landing Distances

DENSITY ALTITUDE CHART

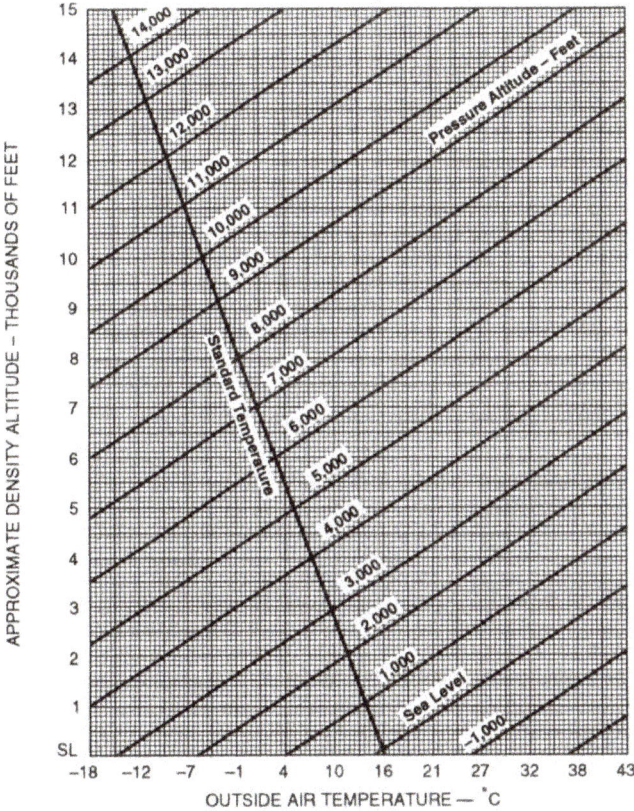

APPROXIMATE DENSITY ALTITUDE – THOUSANDS OF FEET

14,000
13,000
12,000
11,000
10,000
9,000
8,000
7,000
6,000
5,000
4,000
3,000
2,000
1,000
Sea Level
-1,000

Pressure Altitude – Feet

Standard Temperature

OUTSIDE AIR TEMPERATURE — °C
-18 -12 -7 -1 4 10 16 21 27 32 38 43

Altimeter Setting (" Hg)	Pressure Altitude Conversion Factor
28.0	1,824
28.1	1,727
28.2	1,630
28.3	1,533
28.4	1,436
28.5	1,340
28.6	1,244
28.7	1,148
28.8	1,053
28.9	957
29.0	863
29.1	768
29.2	673
29.3	579
29.4	485
29.5	392
29.6	298
29.7	205
29.8	112
29.9	20
29.92	0
30.0	−73
30.1	−165
30.2	−257
30.3	−348
30.4	−440
30.5	−531
30.6	−622
30.7	−712
30.8	−803
30.9	−893
31.0	−983

A RULE YOU CAN LIVE WITH

AOPA Air Safety Institute recommends that you use the 50/50 rule for takeoff correction. That is…

Correcting for altitude and temperature, determine the takeoff distance that's required to clear a 50 foot obstacle. Then, increase that number by an additional 50%.

Higher Density Altitude

There is less thrust:

- Slower takeoff acceleration.
- Longer takeoff rolls.
- Decreased climb rate.

Higher density altitude increases the landing Ground Speed. You'll land at the same indicated airspeed, but because the true airspeed is greater, you'll have a longer landing distance.

Taking Off With a Tailwind

For every 10% of the takeoff speed, a tailwind will increase the ground run by about 21%. **FOR EXAMPLE:** Let's assume that you plan to lift off at 60 knots, and the zero-wind charted takeoff ground roll is 1,300 feet. A 6 knot tailwind, (10% of the 60 knot takeoff speed), will increase your charted 1,300 ground roll by 21%, or 273 feet.

Fickle Headwinds

Winds have a mind of their own, and can change quickly with altitude, or simply disappear. Never count on a headwind to ensure your takeoff!

Crosswinds

The required control surface deflection and tire scrubbing add extra drag, and increase the ground roll.

Exceeding Maximum Takeoff Weight (MTOW)

Excess weight and its consequences:

- Reduced structural load safety factor.
- Reduced acceleration, higher takeoff speed, and longer takeoff distance.
- Reduced rate and angle of climb.
- Reduced cruising speed and range.
- Lower stalling speed and reduced maneuverability.
- Higher landing speed and extended landing distance.
- The aircraft may not leave the ground when you attempt a take-off.

Flight Plan Format

1. Type (VFR, IFR, DVFR)	2. Aircraft ID	3. Aircraft type / Special Equipment	4. TAS
5. Dept Point	6. Dept Time Proposed (Z) Actual (Z)	7. Cruising Alt	
8. Route of Flight			
9. Destination Airport & City	10. ETE	11. Remarks	
12. Fuel On Board (Hours & Minutes)	13. Alternate Airport(s)	14. Pilot's Name, Address & Telephone and Home Base	
15. Number on Board		16. Aircraft Color	
17. Destination Contact/Telephone (Optional)			

To Convert From	To ZULU Time
EST	+5
EDT	+4
CST	+6
CDT	+5
MST	+7
MDT	+6
PST	+8
PDT	+7

See the next page for a list of the *"Most Common General Aviation Special Equipment Suffixes"*.

Most Common General Aviation Special Equipment Suffixes

/X	No Transponder
/T	Transponder, but no Altitude Encoding (Mode C)
/U	Transponder with Mode C
/D	DME, no Transponder
/B	DME& Transponder but no Altitude Encoding (Mode C)
/A	DME & Transponder with Mode C
/I	RNAV or LORAN or INS & Transponder with Mode C
/G	GPS – Enroute & Approach, & Transponder with Mode C

Other books by James D. Price

Flight Review Study Guide will be the first thing you open when getting ready for any pilot proficiency training. Wings or BFR – it's all covered. **Flight Review Study Guide** is also an indispensable cross county flight planning handbook. You'll fly with confidence and you'll be a better pilot.

ISBN 978-1-938586-81-1

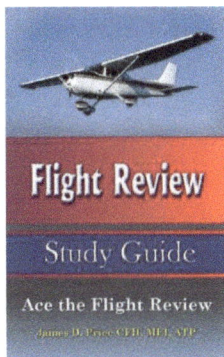

Instrument Proficiency Check Study Guide contains the insight of a professional pilot. Let Jim's training and teaching experiences help you prepare for the IPC. Crack this open any time you need to brush up on your instrument skills and knowledge. It will instill a sense of confidence that only in-depth knowledge can bring. It's a quick and easy way to ACE the IPC.

ISBN 978-1-938586-82-8

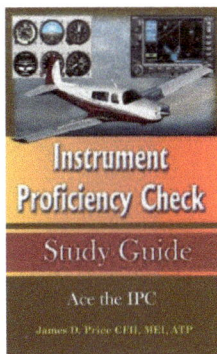

For more information, visit Jim's website at:

http://www.JDPriceCFI.com

Printed in the U.S.A.
http://www.WritersCramp.us